Pirke Avot

Sayings of the Jewish Fathers

Translated by Charles Taylor

Published by Pantianos Classics

ISBN-13: 978-1537634319

This edition was first published in 1897 by Cambridge University Press

Contents

Preface

The Second Edition of Dibré Aboth ha-Olam or Sayings of the Jewish Fathers may be shortly described as a reprint of the work as published in 1877, with a section of ADDITIONAL NOTES. Interspersed with the reprint are insertions in square brackets, a few things are omitted, and short new notes fill up selected pages. With the two titles of the book compare Shebach ABOTH OLAM in the Hebrew of Ecclesiasticus and its Greek rendering Πατέρων ύ?μνος {Greek Patérwn ú?mnos}.

An Appendix not yet published contains the CATALOGUE of Manuscripts referred to in the Introduction, which was announced as undertaken "with especial reference to disputed readings," followed by critical Notes on the Text of Aboth. It is complete as first planned, but awaits a supplement describing

Manuscripts examined or to be examined by Mr Schechter, Reader in Talmudic and Rabbinic in the University of Cambridge, to whose learning and acumen I am indebted for the suggestion of additions and improvements throughout the work.

The collection of Manuscripts lately brought from Egypt by Mr Schechter, with the generous consent of the Grand Rabbi of Cairo, includes some fragments of the Old Testament in Greek with the TETRAGRAMMATON written repeatedly in Hebrew characters ου? το&ιcιρc;ς ν&υcιρc;ν α?λλὰ το&ιcιρc;σ α?ρχαιοτάτοισ {Greek ου? τοῖς νῦν a?llà τοῖς a?rxaiotátois}, in accordance with the remark of Origen on Psalm ii. (Opp. II. 539) that it so stood ε?ν το&ιcιρc;σ α?κριβεστέροισ τω^ν α?ντιγράφων {Greek e?n τοῖς a?kribestérois tw^n a?ntigráfwn}, and the confirmatory testimony of St Jerome (Praef. in Sam. et Malachim) "Et nomen Domini tetragrammaton in quibusdam Graecis voluminibus usque hodie antiquis expressum litteris invenimus." The

Name is so written in the annexed specimen of Aquila's version of the Old Testament (p. viii).

In the same collection is being found more and more of the long lost original Hebrew of ECCLESIASTICUS (p. 169), a book which furnishes not a few apt illustrations of Aboth, although the precise degree of its affinity in thought and diction to the New Hebrew is still under discussion.

Of the innumerable works on ABOTH it must suffice to make mention here of Professor Dr H. L. Strack's concise and thoroughly practical edition Die Sprüche der Väter.

C. TAYLOR

13th August 1897

Introduction

MASSEKETH ABOTH, best known [with the addition of Pereq Rabbi Meir] as Pirqe Aboth, or Chapters of the Fathers, is a Mishnah Tract in Seder Neziqin, where it stands between 'Abodah Zarah and Horaioth. It takes its name from the fact that it consists to a great extent of maxims of the Jewish FATHERS whose names are mentioned in its pages, and is chiefly valued as a compendium of practical ethics, although it is not without a mystical element in portions of its Fifth and concluding Chapter. Its simplicity and intrinsic excellence have secured for ABOTH a widespread and lasting popularity, and have led to its being excerpted from the Talmud and used liturgically in the Synagogue, at certain seasons, from an early period. "It was the custom," writes Sar Shalom Gaon, "in the house of our Rabbi in Babel, to recite ABOTH and (the supplementary sixth chapter) QINYAN THORAH, after evening prayer upon the Sabbath;" and the "Six Chapters" are found at the present day in Prayer Books of the Ashkenazic rite.

The Talmudic saying that Whosoever would be pious must fulfil the dicta of the FATHERS is quoted by Rabbinic commentators in their introductions to Pirqe Aboth, and the Tract has been described, with reference to this saying, as "Mishnath ha-Chasidim," a course of instruction for the pious.

The First Chapter opens with the statement that Moses, having received the Law from Sinai, handed it down to Joshua, and he in turn to the Elders, and the Elders to the men of the Great Synagogue. The Mosaic succession having been thus far established, the men of the Great Synagogue speak their three WORDS, which express the aim and function of the new school of Soferim: "Be deliberate in judgment; and raise up many disciples; and make a hedge to the Law." Next comes Simon Justus, with his saying, that the three pillars of the world are

Revelation, Worship, and Humanity; and after him the first teacher of Greek name, Antigonus, whose inculcation of disinterested service is described in a Jewish tradition as the ultimate source of the negative tenets of the Sadducees, or "Sons of Zadok." From this point onward to the end of the Fourth Chapter we have a series of moral sayings, which are put into the mouths of Rabbis who lived within the period from two centuries before to two centuries after CHRIST.

The Fifth Chapter is characterised by something of a more speculative tendency. It touches upon the cosmogony; upon miracles, and their relation to the order of nature; upon the connexion between the moral and the physical; upon the varieties of men, and minds, and motives; upon the antitheses of the good and the evil dispositions. In form it is a series of groups of ten, seven, four, and three things; its sayings, unlike those in preceding chapters, take the form of historical narrative, or of systematic classification; and it makes no mention of the name of any Mishnah Teacher, until we come, at or near the end, to a saying which is ascribed to Jehudah ben Thema: "Be bold as a leopard, and swift as an eagle, and fleet as a hart, and strong as a lion, to do the will of thy FATHER WHICH IS IN HEAVEN."

Of commentaries upon ABOTH, the best known is that of Maimonides, which is found-- sometimes in the original Arabic, but more commonly in Hebrew--in separate Manuscripts, or in his work on the whole Mishnah, or in Jewish Prayer Books of the Italian rite. Another great commentary, which has been ascribed to R. Jacob ben Shimshon, to R. Shemuel ben Meir, a grandson of Rashi, and even to Rashi himself, is found likewise in separate Manuscripts, and in a great number of Prayer Books, especially of the Franco-German rite. In its most complete form it belongs apparently to the beginning of the thirteenth century, but it is based upon traditions of a much earlier date. A third work which is indispensable for the criticism of ABOTH is the

Arabic commentary of 'R. Israel' of Toledo, which has hitherto been supposed to have perished, except in so far as it was embodied in the Hebrew commentary of his descendant, Isaac ben R. Shelomoh; but a manuscript of R. Israel's work has been lately purchased for the Bodleian Library [1875], and will be found described and identified in [No. 90 of] the forthcoming Catalogue of MANUSCRIPTS OF THE TEXT OF ABOTH AND OF COMMENTARIES UPON IT.

The printed text of the Five Peraqim is from an important manuscript of the MISHNAH, [which was purchased for the Cambridge University Library in 1869, and has been edited by Mr W. H. Lowe, of Christ's College]. The sixth Pereq is taken from a modern Ashkenazic Prayer Book.

The Comparative Index of the Mishnah gives the title of each Tract according to the MS., with its positions in the MS. itself and in the well-known edition of Surenhusius respectively. The Index is followed by extracts from the Mishnah including two complete specimen pages, which, with the exception of the headings, have been transcribed literally and line by line from the MANUSCRIPT. [The Index and the extracts above-mentioned are now transferred to the APPENDIX.]

ST JOHN'S COLLEGE, April 9th, 1877

Chapter I

1. Moses received the Thorah from Sinai, and he delivered it to Jehoshua', and Jehoshua' to the elders, and the elders to the prophets, and the prophets delivered it to the men of the Great Synagogue. They said three things: Be deliberate in judgment; and raise up many disciples; and make a fence to the Thorah.

2. Shime'on ha-Çaddiq was of the remnants of the Great Synagogue. He used to say, On three things the world is stayed; on the Thorah, and on the Worship, and on the bestowal of Kindnesses.

3. Antigonus of Soko received from Shime'on ha-Çaddiq. He used to say, Be not as slaves that minister to the lord with a view to receive recompense; but be as slaves that minister to the lord without a view to receives recompense; and let the fear of Heaven be upon you.

4. Jose ben Jo'ezer of Çeredah and Jose ben Jochanan of Jerusalem received from them. Jose ben Jo'ezer of Çeredah said, Let thy house be a meeting-house for the wise; and powder thyself in the dust of their feet; and drink their words with thirstiness.

5. Jose ben Jochanan of Jerusalem said, Let thy house be opened wide; and let the needy be thy household; and prolong not converse with woman.

6. His own wife, they meant, much less his neighbour's wife.) Hence the wise have said, Each time that the man prolongs converse with the woman he causes evil to himself, and desists from words of Thorah, and in the end he inherits Gehinnom.

7. Jehoshua' ben Perachia and Matthai the Arbelite received from them. Jehoshua' ben Perachiah said, Make unto thyself a master; and possess thyself of an associate; and judge every man in the scale of merit.

8. Matthai the Arbelite said, Withdraw from an evil neighbour; and associate not with the wicked;. and grow not thoughtless of retribution.

9. Jehudah ben Tabai and Shime'on ben Shatach received from them. Jehudah ben Tabai said, Make not thyself as them that predispose the judges; and while the litigants stand before thee, let them be in thine eyes as guilty; and when dismissed from before thee let them be in thine eyes as righteous, because that they have received the doom upon them.

10. Shime'on ben Shatach said, Make full examination of the witnesses; but be guarded in thy words, perchance from them they may learn to lie.

11. Shema'iah and Abtalion received from them. Shema'iah said, Love work; and hate lordship; and make not thyself known to the government.

12. Abtalion said, Ye wise, be guarded in your words; perchance ye may incur the debt of

exile, and be exiled to the place of evil waters; and the disciples that come after you may drink and die, and the Name of Heaven be profaned.

13. Hillel and Shammai received from them. Hillel said, Be of the disciples of Aharon; loving peace, and pursuing peace; loving mankind, and bringing them nigh to the Thorah.

14. He used to say, A name made great is a name destroyed; he who increases not decreases; and he who will not learn (or teach) deserves slaughter; and he who serves himself with the tiara perishes.

15. He used to say, If I am not for myself who is for me? and being for my own self what am I? If not now when?

16. Shammai said, Make thy Thorah an ordinance; say little and do much; and receive every man with a pleasant expression of countenance.

17. Rabban Gamliel said, Make to thyself a master, and be quit of doubt; and tithe not much by estimation.

18. Shime'on his son said, All my days I have grown up amongst the wise, and have not found aught good for a man but silence; not learning but doing is the groundwork; and whoso multiplies words occasions sin.

19. Rabban Shime'on ben Gamliel said, On three things the world stands; on Judgment, and on Truth, and on Peace.

Chapter II

1. Rabbi said, Which is the right course that a man should choose for himself? Whatsoever is a pride to him that pursues it, (and) brings him honour from men. And be attentive to a light precept as to a grave, for thou knowest not the assigned reward of precepts,; and reckon the loss for a duty against its gain, and the gain by a transgression against its loss. And consider three things, and thou wilt not fall into the hands of transgression: know what is above thee-a seeing eye, and a hearing ear, and all thy deeds written in a book.

2. Rabban Gamliel, son of R. Jehudah ha-Nasi, said, Excellent is Thorah study together with worldly business, for the practice of them both puts iniquity out of remembrance; and all Thorah without work must fail at length, and occasion iniquity. And let all who are employed with the congregation act with them in the name of Heaven, for the merit of their fathers

sustains them, and their righteousness stands for ever. And ye yourselves shall have reward reckoned unto you as if ye had wrought.

3. Be cautious with (those in) authority, for they let not a man approach them but for their own purposes; and they appear like friends when it is to their advantage, and stand not by a man in the hour of his need.

4. He used to say, Do His will as if it were thy will, that He may do thy will as if it were His will. Annul thy will before His will, that He may annul the will of others before thy will.

5. Hillel said, Separate not thyself from the congregation, and trust not in thyself until the day of thy death; and judge not thy friend until thou comest into his place; and say not of a word which may be heard that in the end it shall be heard; and say not, When I have leisure I will study; perchance thou mayest not have leisure.

6. He used to say, No boor is a sinfearer; nor is the vulgar pious; nor is the shamefast apt to

learn, nor the passionate to teach; nor is every one that has much traffic wise. And in a place where there are no men endeavour to be a man.

7. Moreover he saw a skull which floated on the face of the water, and he said to it, Because thou drownedst they drowned thee, and in the end they that drowned thee shall be drowned.

8. He used to say, More flesh, more worms: more treasures, more care: more maidservants, more lewdness: more menservants, more theft: more women, more witchcrafts: more Thorah, more life: more wisdom, more scholars: more righteousness, more peace. He who has gotten a good name has gotten it for himself. He who has gotten to himself words of Thorah, has gotten to himself the life of the world to come.

9. Rabban Jochanan ben Zakai received from Hillel and from Shammai. He used to say, If thou hast practised Thorah much, claim not merit to thyself, for thereunto wast thou created.

10. Five disciples were there to Rabban Jochanan 'ben Zakai, and these were they: R. Li'ezer ben Hyrqanos, and R. Jehoshua' ben Chananiah, and R. Jose the Priest, and R. Shime'on ben Nathanael, and R. Ele'azar ben 'Arak. He used to recount their praise: Eli'ezer ben Hyrqanos is a plastered cistern, which loseth not a drop; Jehoshua' ben Chananiah-- happy is she that bare him; Jose the Priest is pious; Shim'eon ben Nathanael is a sinfearer; Ele'azar ben 'Arak is a welling spring.

11. He used to say, If all the wise of Israel were in a scale of the balance, and Eli'ezer ben Hyrqanos in the other scale, he would outweigh them all. Abba Shaul said in his name, If all the wise of Israel were in a scale of the balance, and Eli'ezer ben Hyrqanos with them, and Ele'azar ben 'Arak in the other scale, he would outweigh them all.

12. He said to them, Go and see which Is the good way that a man should cleave to. Rabbi Li'ezer said, A good eye: R. Jehoshua' said, A

good friend: and R. Jose said, A good neighbour: and R. Shime'on said, He that foresees what is to be: R. La'zar said, A good heart. He said to them, I approve the words of Ele'azar ben 'Arak rather than your words, for his words include your words.

13. He said to them, Go and see which is the evil way that a man should shun. R. Li'ezer said, An evil eye: and R. Jehoshua' said, An evil companion: and R. Jose said, An evil neighbour: and R. Shime'on said, He that borroweth and repayeth not--he that borrows from man is the same as if he borrowed from God (blessed is He)--for it is said, The wicked borroweth, and payeth not again, but the righteous is merciful and giveth: R. La'zar said, An evil heart. He said to them, I approve the words of Ele'azar ben 'Arak rather than your words, for your words are included in his words.

14. And they said (each) three things. R. Li'ezer said, Let the honour of thy friend be dear unto thee as thine own; and be not easily provoked;

and repent one day before thy death. And warm thyself before the fire of the wise, but beware of their embers, perchance thou mayest be singed, for their bite is the bite of a fox, and their sting the sting of a scorpion, and their hiss the hiss of a fiery-serpent, and all their words are as coals of fire.

15. R. Jehoshua' said, An evil eye, and the evil nature, and hatred of the creatures put a man out of the world.

16. R. Jose said, Let the property of thy friend be precious unto thee as thine own; set thyself to learn Thorah, for it is not an heirloom unto thee; and let all thy actions be to the name of Heaven.

17. R. Shime'on said, Be careful in reading the Shema' and in Prayer; and when thou prayest, make not thy prayer an ordinance, but an entreaty before God, blessed is He, for it is said, For God is compassionate and easily-entreated, longsuffering, and plenteous in grace; and be not wicked unto thyself.

18. R. La'zar said, Be diligent to learn Thorah, wherewith thou mayest make answer to Epicurus; and know before whom thou toilest; and who is the Master of thy work.

19. R. Tarphon said, The day is short, and the task is great, and the workmen are sluggish, and the reward is much, and the Master of the house is urgent. He said, It is not for thee to finish the work, nor art thou free to desist therefrom; if thou hast learned much Thorah, they give thee much reward; and faithful is the Master of thy work, who will pay thee the reward of thy work, and know that the recompence of the reward of the righteous is for the time to come.

Chapter III

1. 'Aqabiah ben Mahalaleel said, Consider three things, and thou wilt not come into the hands of transgression. Know whence thou camest; and whither thou art going; and before whom thou art about to give account and reckoning. Know whence thou camest: from a fetid drop; and whither thou art going: to worm and maggot; and before whom thou art about to give account and reckoning: before the King of the kings of kings, blessed is He.

2. R. Chananiah, prefect of the priests, said, Pray for the peace of the kingdom, since but for fear thereof we had swallowed up each his neighbour alive.

3. R. Chananiah ben Thradyon said, Two that sit together without words of Thorah are a session of scorners, for it is said, Nor sitteth in the seat of the scornful; but two that sit together and are occupied in words of Thorah have the Shekinah among them, for it is said,

Then they that feared the Lord spake often one to another, &c.

4. One that sits and studies, the Scripture imputes to him as if he fulfilled the whole Thorah, for it is said, He sitteth alone and keepeth silence, because he hath borne it upon him.

5. R. Shime'on said, Three that have eaten at one table, and have not said over it words of Thorah, are as if they had eaten of sacrifices of (the) dead, for it is said, For all tables are full of vomit and filthiness without MAQOM ("without mention of the name of God").

6. But three that have eaten at one table, and have said over it words of Thorah, are as if they had eaten of the table of MAQOM, blessed is He, for it is said, And he said unto me, This is the table that is before the Lord.

7. Chananyiah ben Chakinai said, He who awakes by night, and he who is walking alone by the way, and turns aside his heart to idleness, is "guilty of death."

8. R. Nechonyiah ben ha-Qanah said, Whoso receives upon him the yokel, of Thorah, they remove from him the yoke of royalty and the yoke of worldly care; and whoso breaks from him the yoke of Thorah, they lay upon him the yoke of royalty and the yoke of worldly care.

9. R. Chalaftha of Kaphar-Chananiah said, When ten sit and are occupied in words of Thorah the Shekinah is among them, for it is said, God standeth in the CONGREGATION of the mighty (Ps. lxxxii. 1). And whence (is it proved of) even five? Because! it is said, He judgeth among gods. And whence even three? Because it is said, ... and hath founded his TROOP in the earth (Amos ix. 6). And whence even two? Because it is said, Then they that feared the Lord spake often one to another (§ 3). And whence even one? Because it is said, In all places where I record my name I will come unto THEE, and I will bless thee (Ex. xx. 24).

10. R. La'zar ben Jehudah of Barthotha said, Give Him of what is His, for thou and thine are

His; and thus he saith in David, For all things come of Thee, and of thine own have we given thee (I Chron. xxix. 14).

11. R. Jacob said, He who is walking by the way and studying, and breaks off his study (Mishnah) and says, How fine is this tree! how fine is that tree! and how fine is this fallow? they account it to him as if he were "guilty of death."

12. R. Dosithai, son of R. Jannai, said in the name of R. Meir, When a scholar of the wise sits and studies, and has forgotten a word of his Mishnah, they account it unto him as if he were "guilty of death," for it is said, Only take heed to thyself, and keep thy soul diligently, lest thou forget the words which thine eyes have seen (Deut. iv. 9). Perhaps his Mishnah has but grown hard to him? What need then to say, "And lest they depart from thy heart all the days of thy life"? Lo! he is not guilty, till he has sat down and suffered them to depart from his mind.

13. R. Chananiah ben Dosa said, Whosesoever fear of sin precedes his wisdom, his wisdom stands; and whosesoever wisdom precedes his fear of sin, his wisdom stands not.

14. He used to say, Whosesoever works are in excess ofhis wisdom, his wisdom stands; and whosesoever wisdom is in excess of his works, his wisdom stands not.

15. He used to say, With whomsoever the spirit of men is pleased, the Spirit of God is pleased; and with whomsoever the spirit of men is not pleased, the Spirit of God is not pleased.

16. R. Dosa ben Horkinas said, Morning sleep, and midday wine, and the babbling of youths, and frequenting the meeting houses of the vulgar, put a man out of the world.

17. R. Li'ezer ha-Moda'i said, He that profanes things sacred, and contemns the festivals, and annuls the covenant of Abraham our father, and acts barefacedly against the Thorah, even though he be a doer of good works, has no portion in the world to come.

18. R. Ishma'el said, Be pliant of disposition (or to a chief) and yielding to impressment, and receive every man with cheerfulness.

19. R. 'Aqibah said, Merriment, and lightness of disposition, accustom a man to lewdness.

20. He used to say, Tradition is a fence to Thorah; tithes are a fence to wealth; vows a fence to sanctity; a fence to wisdom is silence.

21. He used to say, Beloved is man that he was created

22. Beloved are Israel that they are called children of God; greater love (was it that it) was made known to them that they are called children of God, as it is said, Ye are the children of the LORD your God (Deut. xiv. 1).

23. Beloved are Israel that there was given to them the instrument with which the world was created; greater love (was it that it) was made known to them that there was given to them the instrument with which the world was created, as it is said, For I give you good doctrine, forsake ye not MY LAW (Prov. iv. 2).

24. Everything is foreseen; and freewill is given. And the world is judged by grace; and everything is according to work.

25. He used to say, Everything is given on pledge; and the net (Eccl. ix. 12) is cast over all the living. The office is open; and the broker gives credit; and the ledger is open; and the hand writes; and whosoever will borrow comes and borrows; and the bailiffs go round continually every day, and exact from a man whether he wills or not; and they have whereon to lean; and the judgment is a judgment of truth. And everything is prepared for the BANQUET.

26. R. La'zar ben 'Azariah said, No Thorah, no culture; no culture, no Thorah. No wisdom, no fear (of God); no fear (of God), no wisdom. No knowledge, no discernment; no discernment, no knowledge. No meal, no Thorah; no Thorah, no meal.

27. He used to say, Whosesoever wisdom is in excess of his works, to what is he like? To a tree

whose branches are abundant, and its roots scanty; and the wind comes, and uproots it, and overturns it. And whosesoever works are in excess of his wisdom, to what is he like? To a tree whose branches are scanty, and its roots abundant; though all the winds come upon it, they stir it not from its place.

28. R. La'zar Chasmah said, "Qinnim" (Mishnah about bird-sacrifices) and "Pitheché Niddah" (Mishnah relating to menstruation) are essentials of Thorah; canons of astronomy and Gematria (Numerology) are after courses of wisdom.

Chapter IV

1. Ben Zoma said, Who is wise? He that learns from every man; for it is said, From all my teachers I gat understanding (Ps. cxix. 99).

2. Who is mighty? He that subdues his nature; for it is said, He that is slow to anger is better than the mighty; and he that ruleth his spirit than he that taketh a city (Prov. xvi. 32).

3. Who is rich? He that is contented with his lot; for it is said, When thou eatest the labour of thy hands, happy art thou, and it shall be well with thee (Ps. cxxviii. 2). "Happy art thou" in this world; "and it shall be well with thee" in the world to comes.

4. Who is honoured? He that honours mankind; for it is said, For them that honour me I will honour, and they that despise me shall be lightly esteemed (I Sam. ii. 30).

5. Ben 'Azzai said, Hasten to a slight precept, and flee from transgression; for precept

induces precept, and transgression induces transgression; for the reward of precept is precept, and the reward of transgression is transgression.

6. He used to say, Despise not any man, and carp not at any thing; for thou wilt find that there is not a man that has not his hour, and not a thing that has not its place.

7. R. Levitas of Jabneh said, Be exceeding lowly of spirit, for the hope of man is the worm. R. Jochanan ben Baroqah said, Whoso profanes the name of Heaven in secret, they punish him openly. The erring is as the presumptuous, in profanation of the NAME.

8. R. Ishma'el his son said, He that learns in order to teach, they grant him the faculty to learn and to teach: he that learns in order to practise, they grant him the faculty to learn, and to teach, and to practise.

9. R. Çadoq said, Make them not a crown, to glory in them; nor an ax, to live by them. And thus was Hillel wont to say, And he who serves

himself with the tiara perishes. Lo, whosoever makes profit from words of Thorah removes his life from the world.

10. R. Jose said, Whosoever honours the Thorah is himself held in honour with men; and whosoever dishonours the Thorah is himself dishonoured with men.

11. R. Ishma'el said, He that refrains himself from judgment, frees himself from enmity, and rapine, and false swearing; and he that is arrogant in decision is foolish, wicked, and puffed up in spirit.

12. He used to say, Judge not alone, for none may judge alone save One; and say not, Accept ye my opinion, for they are free-to-choose, and not thou.

13. R. Jochanan said, Whosoever fulfils the Thorah in poverty, will at length fulfil it in wealth; and whosoever neglects the Thorah in wealth, will at length neglect it in poverty.

14. R. Meir said, Have little business, and be busied in Thorah; and be lowly in spirit unto

every man; and if thou idlest from the Thorah, thou wilt have idlers many against thee; and if thou labourest in the Thorah, He hath much reward to give unto thee.

15. R. Li'ezer ben Jacob said, He who performs one precept has gotten to himself one advocate; and he who commits one transgression has gotten to himself one accuser. Repentance and good works are as a shield against punishment.

16. R. Jochanan Sandalarius said, Whatsoever assemblage is in the name of duty will in the end be established; and that which is not in the name of duty will not in the end be established.

17. R. La'zar said, Let the honour of thy disciple be dear unto thee as the honour of thine associate; and the honour of thine associate as the fear of thy master; and the fear of thy master as the fear of Heaven.

18. R. Jehudah said, Be careful in Thalmud, for error in Thalmud amounts to sin.

19. R. Shime'on said, There are three crowns: the crown of Thorah, and the crown of Priesthood, and the crown of Royalty (Ex. xxv. 10, 11; xxx. 1, 3; xxv. 23, 24); but the crown of a good name mounts above them (Eccl. vii. 1).

20. R. Nehorai said, Betake thyself to a place of Thorah, and say not that it shall come after thee; for thine associates will confirm it unto thee; and lean not unto thine own understanding (Prov. iii. 5).

21. R. Jannai said, Neither the security of the wicked, nor the afflictions of the righteous, are in our hand.

22. R. Matthiah ben Charash said, Be beforehand in saluting every man; and be a tail to lions, and not a head to foxes.

23. R. Jacob said, This world is like a vestibule before the world to come; prepare thyself at the vestibule, that thou mayest be admitted into the hall.

24. He used to say, Better is one hour of repentance and good works in this world than

all the life of the world to come; better is one hour of refreshment of spirit in the world to come than all the life of this world.

25. R. Shime'on ben Ele'azar said, Conciliate not thy friend in the hour of his passion; and console him not in the hour when his dead is laid out before him; and "interrogate" him not in the hour of his vow; and strive not to see him in the hour of his disgrace.

26. Shemuel ha-Qatan said, Rejoice not when thine enemy falleth, and let not thine heart be glad when he stumbleth (Prov. xxiv. 17).

27. Elisha' ben Abiyyah said, He who learns as a lad, to what is he like? to ink written on fresh paper; and he who learns when old, to what is he like? to ink written on used paper.

28. R. Jose ben Jehudah of Kaphar ha-Babli said, He who learns from the young, to what is he like? to one that eats unripe grapes, and drinks wine from his vat; and he who learns from the old, to what is he like? to one that eats ripened grapes, and drinks old wine.

29. R. said, Regard not the flask, but what is therein; there is a new flask that is full of old (wine), and an old one in which there is not even new.

30. R. Li'ezer ha-Qappar said, Jealousy, and lust, and ambition, put a man out of the world.

31. He used to say, The born are to die; and the dead to revive; and the living to be judged; for to know, and to notify, and that it may be known, that He is the framer, and He the creator, and He the discerner, and He the judge, and He the witness, and He the "adversary," and He is about to judge with whom there is no iniquity, nor forgetfulness, nor respect of persons, nor taking of a bribe, for all is His, and know that all is according to plan.

32. Let not thine imagination assure thee that the grave is an asylum; for perforce thou wast framed (Jer. xviii. 6), and perforce thou wast born, and perforce thou livest, and perforce thou diest, and perforce thou art about to give

account and reckoning before the King of the kings of kings, the Holy One, blessed is He.

Chapter V

1. By ten Sayings the world was created. And what is learned therefrom? for could it not have been created by one Saying? But it was that vengeance might be taken on the wicked, who destroy the world that was created by ten Sayings; and to give a goodly reward to the righteous, who maintain the world that was created by ten Sayings.

2. Ten generations were there from Adam to Noach, to shew how great was His longsuffering; for all the generations were provoking Him, till He brought the deluge upon them.

3. Ten generations were there from Noach to Abraham, to shew how great was His longsuffering; for all the generations were provoking Him, till Abraham our father came, and received the reward of them all.

4. With ten temptations was Abraham our father tempted, and he withstood them all; to

shew how great was the love of Abraham our father.

5. Ten miracles were wrought for our fathers in Egypt; and ten by the sea.

6. Ten plagues brought the Holy One, blessed is He, upon the Egyptians in Egypt; and ten by the Sea.

7. With ten temptations did our fathers tempt God in the wilderness, for it is said, And they have tempted me now these ten times, and have not hearkened to my voice (Numb. xiv. 22).

8. Ten miracles were wrought in the Sanctuary. No woman miscarried from the scent of the holy meat; and the holy meat never stank; and an uncleanness befel not the highpriest on the day of the Atonement; and a fly was not seen in the slaughterhouse; and a defect was not found in the sheaf; nor in the two loaves; nor in the shewbread; and rains quenched not the pile; and the wind prevailed not against the pillar of smoke; they stood serried, and bowed down at

ease; and serpent and scorpion harmed not in Jerusalem; and a man said not to his fellow, The place is too strait for me (Is. xlix. 20) to lodge in Jerusalem.

9. Ten things were created between the suns. The mouth of the earth; and the mouth of the well; and the mouth of the ass; and the bow (Gen. lx. 13); and the manna; and the rod (a rod of power given to Adam, passed down to Joseph and eventually to Pharaoh; Moses alone could read the letters on it); and the shamir-worm (a magical worm Moses used to engrave the tablets of the law and split stones); and the character; and the writing; and the tables. And some say, the spirits also; and the sepulchre of Moses (Deut. xxxiv. 6); and the ram of Abraham our father (Gen. xxii. 13). And some say, tongs also, made with tongs.

10. Seven things are in a clod, and seven in a wise man. The wise man speaks not before one who is greater than he in wisdom; and does not interrupt the words of his companion; and is

not hasty to reply; he asks according to canon, and answers to the point; and speaks on the first thing first, and on the last last; of what he has not heard he says, I have not heard; and he acknowledges the truth. And their opposites are in the clod.

11. Seven kinds of punishments come on account of seven main transgressions. When some men tithe, and some do not tithe, dearth from drought comes: some of them are hungry, and some of them are full. When they have not tithed at all, a dearth from tumult and from drought comes. And when they have not offered the dough-cake, a deadly dearth comes.

12. Pestilence comes into the world for the capital crimes mentioned in the Thorah, which are not brought before the tribunal; and for the seventh year fruits.

13. The sword comes upon the world for suppression of judgment; and for perversion of judgment; and for explaining Thorah not according to canon.

14. Noisome beasts come into the world for vain swearing; and for profanation of the NAME.

Captivity comes upon the world for strange worship; and for incest; and for shedding of blood; and for (not) giving release to the land.

15. At four seasons the pestilence waxes: in the fourth (year); in the seventh; at the ending of the seventh; and at the ending of the Feast in every year. In the fourth (year), on account of the poor's tithe in the third; in the seventh, on account of the poor's tithe in the sixth; and at the ending of the seventh, on account of the seventh year fruits; and at the ending of the Feast in every year,, on account of the largesses of the poor.

16. There are four characters in men, He that saith, Mine is mine, and thine is thine, is an indifferent character; but some say, It is the character of Sodom: (he that saith) Mine is thine, and thine is mine, is 'am ha-areç: Mine

and thine are thine, pious: Thine and mine are mine, wicked.

17. There are four characters in dispositions. Easily provoked, and easily pacified, his gain is cancelled by his loss: hard to provoke and hard to pacify, his loss is cancelled by his gain: hard to provoke, and easily pacified, pious: easily provoked, and hard to pacify, wicked.

18. There are four characters in scholars. Quick to hear and quick to forget, his gain is cancelled by his loss: slow to hear and slow to forget, his loss is cancelled by his gain: quick to hear, and slow to forget, is wise: slow to hear, and quick to forget, this is an evil lot.

19. There are four characters in almsgivers. He who is willing to give, but not that others should give, his eye is evil towards the things of others: that others should give, and he should not give, his eye is evil towards his own: he who would give and let others give, is pious: he who will not give nor let others give, is wicked.

20. There are four characters in college-goers. He that goes and does not practise, the reward of going is in his hand: he that practises and does not go, the reward of practice is in his hand: he that goes and practises is pious: he that goes not and does not practise is wicked.

21. There are four characters in those who sit under the wise; a sponge; a funnel; a strainer; and a bolt-sieve. A sponge, which sucks up all; a funnel, which lets in here and lets out there; a strainer, which lets out the wine and keeps back the dregs; a bolt-sieve, which lets out the pollard and keeps back the flour.

22. All love which depends on some thing, when the thing ceases, the love ceases; and such as does not depend on anything, ceases not for ever.

23. What love is that which depends on some thing? the love of Amnon and Thamar; And that which does not depend on anything? this is the love of David and Jonathan.

24. Whatsoever gainsaying is for the name of Heaven will in the end be established; and that which is not for the name of Heaven will not in the end be established.

25. What gainsaying is that which is for the name of Heaven? the gainsaying of Shammai and Hillel. And that which is not for the name of Heaven? this is the gainsaying of Qorach.

26. Whosoever makes the many righteous, sin prevails not over him; and whosoever makes the many to sin, they grant him not the faculty to repent.

27. Moses was righteous, and made the many righteous, and the righteousness of the many was laid upon him, for it is said, He executed the justice of the Lord and His judgments, WITH Israel (Deut. xxxiii. 21). Jerobe'am sinned, and caused the many to sin, (and) the sin of the many was laid upon him, for it is said, Because of the sins of Jerobe'am who sinned, and made Israel to sin (I Kings xiv. 16, &c.).

28. In whomsoever are three things, he is a disciple of Abraham; and three (other) things, a disciple of Bile'am.

29. A good eye, and a lowly soul, and a humble spirit (belong to) the disciple of Abraham: an evil eye, and a swelling soul, and a haughty spirit, to the disciple of Bile'am. And what difference is between the disciples of Abraham and the disciples of Bile'am? The disciples of Bile'am, go down to Gehinnom, for it is said, But thou, O God, shalt bring them down into the pit of destruction (Ps. lv. 24), but the disciples of Abraham inherit the Garden of 'Eden, for it is said, That I may cause those that love me to inherit SUBSTANCE; and I will fill their treasures (Prov. viii. 21).

30. R. Jehudah ben Thema said, Be bold as a leopard, and swift as an eagle, and fleet as a hart, and strong as a lion, to do the will of thy Father which is in Heaven.

31. He used to say, The bold of face to Gehinnom; and the shamefaced to the garden

of 'Eden. May it be well-pleasing in thy sight, Lord, our God, and the God of our fathers, that thy city may be built in our days; and give us our portion in thy Thorah.

32. Ben Bag-bag said, Turn it, and again turn it; for the all is therein, and thy all is therein: and swerve not therefrom, for thou canst have no greater excellency than this.

33. Ben He-he said, According to the toil is the reward.

Addenda - The Ages of Man

He used to say, At five years old, Scripture: at ten years, Mishnah: at thirteen, the Commandments: at fifteen, Thalmud: at eighteen, the bridal: at twenty, pursuits: at thirty, strength: at forty, discernment: at fifty, counsel: at sixty, age: at seventy, hoariness: at eighty, power: at ninety, decrepitude: at a hundred, it is as though he were dead, and gone, and had ceased from the world.

Chapter VI - Pereq R. Meir - On the Acquisition of Thorah

All Israel have a portion in the world to come, for it is said, Thy people also shall be all righteous: they shall inherit the land for ever, the branch of my planting, the work of my hands, that I may be glorified (Sanhedrin xi. 1; Isaiah Ix. 21).

Wise men have taught in the Mishnah tongue; blessed is He that made choice of them and their Mishnah:

1. RABBI MEIR said, Whosoever is busied in Thorah for its own sake merits many things; and not only so, but he is worth the whole world: he is called friend, beloved: loves God, loves mankind: pleases God, pleases mankind. And it clothes him with meekness and fear, and fits him to become righteous, pious, upright and faithful: and removes him from sin, and

brings him toward the side of merit. And they enjoy from him counsel, and sound wisdom, understanding, and strength, for it is said, Counsel is mine, and sound wisdom: I am understanding; I have strength (Prov, viii. 14). And it gives him kingdom, and dominion, and faculty of judgment. And they reveal to him the secrets of Thorah; and he is made, as it were, a spring that ceases not, and as a river that flows on increasing. And he becomes modest, and long-suffering, and forgiving of insult. And it magnifies him and exalts him over all things.

2. Said Rabbi Jehoshua' ben Levi, Every day Bath Qol goes forth from Mount Choreb, and makes proclamation and says, Woe to the creatures for contempt of Thorah, for whosoever does not occupy himself in Thorah is called "blameworthy," for it is said, As a jewel of gold in a swine's snout, so is a fair woman which is without discretion (Prov. xi. 22). And it saith, And the tables were the work of God, and the writing was the writing of God, graven upon the tables (Ex. xxxii. 16); read not

CHARUTH, graven, but CHERUTH, freedom, for thou wilt find no freeman but him who is occupied in learning of Thorah; and whosoever is occupied in learning of Thorah, behold he exalts himself, for it is said, And from Matthanah to Nachaliel: and from Nachaliel to Bamoth (Numb. xxi. 19).

3. He who learns from his companion one section, or one canon, or one verse, or one word, (or) even one letter, is bound to do him honour; for thus we find with David king of Israel, who learned not from Achithophel but two things only, that he called him his master, his guide, and his acquaintance,

for it is said, But it was thou, a man mine equal, my guide, and mine acquaintance (Ps. lv. 14). And is there not an argument from the greater to the less, that as David king of Israel, who learned not from Achithophel but two words only, called him his master, his guide, and his acquaintance, he who learns from his companion one section, or one canon, or one verse, or one word, or even one letter, is so many times the more bound to do him honour? And honour is nothing but Thorah, for it is said, The wise shall inherit honour (Prov. iii. 35). And the perfect shall inherit good (Prov. xxviii. 10). And good is nothing but Thorah, for it is said, For I give you good doctrine, forsake ye not my Thorah (Prov. iv. 2).

4. This is the path of Thorah: A morsel with salt (This is a Talmudic phrase for a poor man's fare--Berakoth 2 b), shalt thou eat; Thou shalt drink also water by measure (Ezek. iv. 11); and shalt sleep upon the ground, and live a life of painfulness, and in Thorah shalt thou labour. If thou doest thus, Happy shalt thou be, and it shall be well with thee (Ps. cxxviii. 2): "happy shalt thou be" in this world; "and it shall be well with thee "in the world to come.

5. Seek not greatness for thyself, and desire not honour. Practise more than thou learnest. And lust not for the table of kings, for thy table is greater than their table, and thy crown greater

than their crown, and faithful is thy task-master who will pay thee the wage of thy work.

6. Greater is Thorah than the priesthood, and than the kingdom; for the kingdom is acquired by thirty degrees, and the priesthood by four and twenty, and the Thorah is acquired by forty and eight things. And these are they, by learning, by a listening ear, by ordered speech, by discernment of heart, by dread, by fear, by meekness, by cheerfulness, by pureness, by attendance upon the wise, by discussion with associates, by the argumentation of disciples, by sedateness; by Scripture, by Mishnah; by little traffic, by little intercourse, by little luxury, by little sleep, by little converse, by little merriment; by long-suffering, by a good heart, by faith in the wise, by acceptance of chastisements; he that knows his place, and that rejoices in his portion, and that makes a fence to his words, and does not claim merit to himself; he is loved, loves God, loves mankind, loves righteousnesses, loves uprightness, loves reproofs; and retires from honour, and puffs

not up his heart with his learning, and is not forward in decision; bears the yoke with his associate, and inclines him to the scale of merit, and grounds him upon the truth, and grounds him upon peace; and settles his heart to his study; asks and answers, hears and adds thereto; he that learns in order to teach, and that learns in order to practise; that makes his master wiser, and that considers what he has heard, and that tells a thing in the name of him that said it. Lo, thou hast learned that whosoever tells a thing in the name of him that said it, brings redemption to the world, for it is said, And Esther told it to the king in the name of Mordekai (Esth. ii. 22).

7. Great is Thorah, which gives life to those who practise it in this world and in the world to come, for it is said, For they are life unto those that find them, and health to all their flesh (Prov. iv. 22); and it saith, It shall be health to thy navel, and marrow to thy bones (Prov. iii. 8); and it saith, She is a tree of life to them that lay hold upon her: and happy is

every one that retaineth her (Prov. iii. 18); and it saith, For they shall be an ornament of grace unto thy head, and chains about thy neck (Prov. i. 9); and it saith, She shall give to thine head an ornament of grace: a crown of glory shall she deliver to thee (Prov. iv. 9); and it saith, For by me thy days shall be multiplied, and the years of thy life shall be increased (Prov. ix. 11); and it saith, Length of days is in her right hand; and in her left hand riches and honour (Prov. iii. 16): and it saith, For length of days, and years of life, and peace, shall they add to thee (Prov. iii. 2).

8. Rabbi Shime'on ben Jehudah, in the name of Rabbi Shime'on ben Jochai, said, Comeliness, and strength, and wealth, and honour, and wisdom, and age, and hoariness, and sons, are comely to the righteous, and comely to the world, for it is said, The hoary head is a crown of glory; it is found in the way of righteousness (Prov. xvi. 31); and it saith, The glory of young men is their strength: and the

beauty of old men is the grey head (Prov. xx. 29); and it saith, Sons' sons are the crown of old men; and the glory of sons are their fathers (Prov. xvii. 6); and it saith, Then the moon shall be confounded, and the sun ashamed, when the Lord of hosts shall reign in mount Zion, and in Jerusalem, and before his ancients gloriously (Is. xxiv. 23).

Rabbi Shime'on ben Manasia said, These (?) seven qualities which the wise have reckoned to the righteous were all of them confirmed in Rabbi and his sons.

9. Said Rabbi Jose ben Qisma, Once I was walking by the way, and there met me a man, and be gave me "Peace"; and I returned him "Peace." He said to me, Rabbi, from what place art thou? I said to him, From a great city of wise men, and doctors, am I. He said to me, Rabbi, should it be thy pleasure to dwell with us in our place, I will give thee a thousand thousand dinars of gold, and goodly stones, and pearls. I said to him, If thou shouldest give me

all the silver, and gold, and goodly stones, and pearls that are in the world, I would not dwell but in a place of Thorah; and thus it is written in the book of Psalms, by the hands of David, king of Israel, The law of thy mouth is better unto me than thousands of gold and silver (Ps. cxix. 72). Moreover in the hour of a man's decease not silver, nor gold, nor goodly stones, and pearls accompany the man, but Thorah and good works alone, for it is said, When thou goest, it shall lead thee; when thou sleepest, it shall keep thee; and when thou awakest, it shall talk with thee (Prov. vi. 22). "When thou goest, it shall lead thee," in this world: "when thou sleepest, it shall keep thee," in the grave: "and when thou awakest, it shall talk with thee," in the world to come. And it saith, The silver is mine, and the gold is mine, saith the Lord of hosts (Hang. ii. 8).

10. Five, possessions possessed the Holy One, blessed is He, in his world, and these are they: THORAH, one possession; HEAVEN AND EARTH, one possession; Abraham, one

possession; ISRAEL, one possession; THE SANCTUARY, one possession. Thorah, whence? because it is written, The Lord possessed me in the beginning of his way, before his works of old (Prov. viii. 22); Heaven and Earth, whence? because it is written, Thus saith the Lord, The heaven is my throne, and the earth is my footstool: where is the house that ye build unto me? and where is the place of my rest (Is. lxvi. 1)? and it saith, O Lord, how manifold are thy works! in wisdom hast thou made them all: the earth is full of thy possessions (Ps. civ. 24); Abraham, whence? because it is written, And he blessed him, and said, Blessed be Abram of the most high God, possessor of heaven and earth (Gen. xiv. 19); Israel, whence? because it is written, Till thy people pass over, O Lord, till the people pass over, which thou hast possessed (Ex. xv. 16); and it saith, To the saints that are in the earth, and to the excellent, in whom is all my delight (Ps. xvi. 3); The Sanctuary, whence? because it is written, The place, O Lord, which thou hast made for thee to dwell in, the sanctuary, O Lord, which thy hands have established (Ex. xv. 17); and it saith, And he brought them to the border of his sanctuary, even to this mountain, which his right-hand had possessed (Ps. lxxviii. 54).

11. Whatsoever the Holy One, blessed is He, created in his world, he created not but for his glory, for it is said, Every one that is called by my name: for I have created him for my glory, I have formed him; yea, I have made him (Is. xliii. 7); and it saith, The Lord shall reign for ever and ever (Ex. xv. 18).

Rabbi Chanania ben 'Aqashia said, The Holy One, blessed is He, was pleased to give merit to Israel: therefore he multiplied unto them Thorah and precepts, for it is said, The Lord is well pleased for his righteousness' sake; he will magnify the law, and make it honourable (Is. xlii. 21).

Manufactured by Amazon.ca
Bolton, ON